Crazy Creatures

OF AUSTRALIA AND NEW ZEALAND

BY JOANNE MATTERN

Perfection Learning®

BOOK DESIGN: Jan M. Michalson

ABOUT THE AUTHOR

Joanne Mattern is the author of many books for children. Her favorite topics include animals, biography, and history. She especially likes writing nonfiction because it allows her to bring real people, places, and events to life. "I firmly believe that everything in the world is a story waiting to be told."

Along with writing, Joanne enjoys speaking to school and community groups about the topics in her books. She is also a huge baseball fan and enjoys music and needlework.

Joanne lives in the Hudson Valley of New York State with her husband and young daughter. The family also includes a greyhound and two cats, and "more animals are always welcome!"

IMAGE CREDITS

Cover and Title Page Image Credits
Left from top to bottom: Corel, www.arttoday.com, Digital Stock, Digital Stock, Digital Stock, Corbis. Right: Corel.

Insides Image Credits
Corel: pp. 3, 4, 5, 6, 7, 8, 14, 15, 17, 26–27, 28, 30 left, 31, 33 background, 36, 44, 46, 48, 50, 52, 56. www.arttoday.com: pp. 9, 10, 11, 24, 30 right, 33 center, 56. ANT Photo Library: pp. 12, 16, 18, 19, 20, 21, 25, 35, 38–39, 45, 49. Corbis: pp. 13, 53, 54. aussieSTOCK.com.au: pp. 22, 29, 32, 34, 42, 43. Digital Stock: pp. 40, 41. koura.co.nz: p. 55.

4 5 6 7 8 9 PP 10 09 08 07 06 05

Contents

Chapter 1

Australia and New Zealand

Our planet has seven continents. But only one is an island. That island continent is called Australia. East of Australia is a group of islands called New Zealand.

Many animals live on Australia and New Zealand. Most of them aren't found anywhere else in the world. And many animals that live in other countries don't live there.

That means that Australia and New Zealand are home to some of the craziest creatures on Earth!

Chapter 2

Australia's Marsupials

The weirdest animals that live in Australia are called *marsupials*. Marsupials are mammals. Mammals are warm-blooded. Their bodies are covered with hair or fur. They give birth to live young and nurse them with milk.

You are a mammal too. However, marsupials are very different from you!

At birth, marsupial babies are very tiny. They're not able to live on their own. So the babies crawl into pouches on their mothers' stomachs. The babies stay in these pouches for several weeks or months. By then, they are big enough to survive outside.

Let's meet some of these crazy marsupials!

Kangaroos

Do you like to jump? Kangaroos do! Kangaroos can leap more than 30 feet in one jump. They have long, strong back legs.

Kangaroos are more than 6 feet long. Their tails are more than 3 feet long. Kangaroos use their long tails to keep their balance when they jump. They also sit on them, just as you might sit on a stool!

Baby kangaroos are called *joeys*. Joeys are about the size of lima beans when they are born. They quickly crawl into their mothers' pouches. They stay there for about 6 months. Later, they still stick their heads back into the pouches to nurse. Joeys also climb in when they are scared or want to be close to their mothers.

Tree Kangaroos

There are many different kinds of kangaroos. The bodies of tree kangaroos are only 2½ feet long. But their tails are about 3 feet long.

Just like their bigger cousins, these little kangaroos like to jump. They often jump from one tree branch to another. They use their long tails for balance.

Tree kangaroos also have special feet and claws. Rough pads on their feet help them cling to branches. And their curved claws help them climb.

Pademelons

Pademelons are another type of small kangaroo. Large groups live in underground tunnels. If they sense danger, they thump the ground with their back legs. Then they dive underground for safety.

Koalas

Does it sound crazy to eat only one type of food? Koalas don't think so! Koalas eat only the leaves of eucalyptus trees. Koalas have special pouches in their cheeks to store leaves while they chew.

Koalas live in a part of Australia that is very dry and hot. So they hardly ever drink water. They get what they need from the leaves.

Koalas don't just eat from eucalyptus trees. They live in them too! These furry little animals spend almost all their time in the trees, eating and sleeping.

Wombats

Three kinds of wombats are found in Australia. Two kinds have noses covered with long hair. The third kind has a smooth nose.

Like many marsupials, wombats are *nocturnal*. This means they hunt at night when the air is cooler.

Numbats

Unlike most marsupials, numbats are active during the day. They dig into rotten logs, looking for termites and ants to eat. They slurp up the insects with their long tongues.

Numbats don't have deep pouches like other marsupials do. Instead, baby numbats hold on to hollow spots on their mothers' undersides. The babies have to hang on tight to the fur or they'll fall off!

Numbats have about 50 teeth. That's more than any other land mammal.

Bandicoots

Several different types of bandicoots live in Australia. These small marsupials have brown or gray fur, long tails, and short legs. And they have long, strong, crazy claws!

Some bandicoots use their claws to dig underground homes up to 6 feet deep. They also use their long claws to dig up earthworms to eat.

Like most marsupials, female bandicoots carry their babies in pouches on their stomachs. But bandicoots' pouches face backward. This may sound crazy, but it's not! Dirt can't get in the pouches when bandicoots dig.

Tasmania is an island southeast of Australia. That's where Tasmanian devils live.

These large marsupials will eat almost anything. They kill smaller animals for food. They also *scavenge*, or eat, animals that are already dead.

Tasmanian devils eat every part of their prey—even the fur and the bones. They crush the bones with their powerful teeth.

Despite their scary name, Tasmanian devils are very shy. They are scared of people. Their name comes from the weird, whining sounds they make when they are angry.

Thylacines

Thylacines look very strange! Their feet and teeth look like those of dogs. They whine, bark, and growl like dogs too. But these animals have stripes on their backs like tigers. And they live on Tasmania. That's why they are also called Tasmanian wolves and Tasmanian tigers.

Thylacines hunt rats, birds, and other small animals.

Usually they walk on all four legs. But if they are frightened, thylacines hop away on their back legs like kangaroos. Does that sound crazy to you?

Here's another crazy thing about thylacines. No one knows if they're still around. Nobody has seen one for many years. But some people think these animals still live in places where people don't visit.

Sugar Gliders

Imagine gliding through the air. That's what sugar gliders do! These animals have webs of skin between their front and back legs. These webs help sugar gliders "fly" from tree to tree. They can travel up to 164 feet in one jump!

Sugar gliders live in eucalyptus trees. Their main foods are nectar, fruit, and eucalyptus sap.

Feathertail Gliders

Like sugar gliders, feathertail gliders have webs of skin between their arms and legs. Feathertails spread their webs to glide from tree to tree.

Feathertail gliders get their name from their funny-looking tails. They have rows of stiff hairs on the sides of their tails. These hairs look like feathers.

Cuscuses are a type of opossum. They climb through trees at night, eating leaves and fruit.

Cuscuses have crazy feet that are just right for life in the trees. Their back feet have clawless big toes that face the rest of the foot. Their toes help the animals grip branches.

Cuscuses' tails are also pretty weird. They have *prehensile* tails. This means their tails are almost like hands. Cuscuses can hang by their tails from tree branches. Or they can use their tails to grab things.

Planigales

Planigales look like tiny kangaroos. They weigh less than an ounce and are just 5 inches long. These little animals are the smallest marsupials.

Even though planigales are small, they are very fast! They hop quickly on their long back legs.

Planigales come out at night to hunt grasshoppers. But often that's a problem. Grasshoppers can be bigger than planigales! Still, these little hunters are able to catch and eat the larger insects.

Mulgaras

Mulgaras have big appetites! They run after mice, birds, and small lizards. They can eat up to 25 percent of their own weight every day.

Mulgaras live where it's hot and dry. They hardly ever drink water. Instead, they get most of the water they need from their food.

These animals stay in their underground homes until the sun goes down. That's not crazy. That's smart!

Fat-tailed dunnarts are very small mice. Killing the crickets and grasshoppers they eat is hard because of their small size. But they are small enough to slip into narrow places. This helps them escape predators.

After fat-tailed dunnarts eat, they store some of the food as fat in their tails. If they can't find food later, they live off the stored fat. After they use all the fat, their tails become thin again.

Marsupial Moles

These moles have no eyes! They don't need them. They spend their lives underground.

Marsupial moles dig tunnels with their long claws. Then they hunt earthworms and insects.

The moles' bodies are only 6 inches long. They are shaped like ovals. The oval shape helps them move through narrow tunnels. Hard coverings over their noses protect them from dirt and sand.

Chapter 3

More Strange Mammals

Platypuses

Platypuses just might be the craziest animals in the world! Scientists were shocked when they first saw them. They thought somebody had sewn together parts of different animals as a joke.

Platypuses have webbed feet and beaks like ducks. They have flat tails like beavers. And their long, furry bodies look like otters.

Their looks aren't the only crazy things about platypuses. They are also one of only two mammals in the world that lay eggs. The other egg-laying mammals are echidnas. They also live in Australia.

As if laying eggs weren't strange enough, platypuses are the only mammals that have venom. Adult males have long, sharp spurs filled with venom on the insides of their back legs. They use these poisonous spurs as weapons when they fight.

Echidnas

Echidnas are mammals. But unlike most mammals, they lay eggs. Platypuses are the only other mammals that lay eggs.

Echidnas and platypuses belong to a special group of mammals called *monotremes*. Monotreme means "egg-laying mammal."

Echidnas' backs are covered with long, sharp spikes. The spikes protect them from enemies. If echidnas are in danger, they dig into the ground. Or they roll themselves into balls to protect their faces and bodies.

Echidnas are also called "spiny anteaters." They like to eat ants and termites. They dig into these insects' nests. Then they use their sticky tongues to lick up the food.

False Vampire Bats

These big bats aren't really vampires. They don't suck blood from their prey. But they do eat other animals.

False vampire bats nest in hollow trees. The bottoms of the trees are often covered with the blood and bones of the bats' prey.

 CHapter 4

Birds

Birds are the only animals that have feathers. Feathers help birds fly. Most birds can fly. But a few cannot. They are too heavy. There are several birds in Australia and New Zealand that cannot fly.

Birds are *vertebrates*. That means they have backbones. Most birds' bones are hollow. So birds are very light. This helps them fly.

Birds do not give birth to live young. Instead, they lay eggs. Baby birds, or *chicks*, develop inside the eggs.

Australia and New Zealand are home to some very unusual birds. Let's meet some.

Emus

Emus can't fly. But that doesn't mean they can't move fast! Emus are great runners. Their long legs and strong feet help them run up to 30 miles per hour.

Emus are the second largest birds in the world. They grow up to 6½ feet tall. Their size is the reason they can't fly. Their bodies are just too heavy to get off the ground!

Usually, female animals take care of their babies. But male emus are the main caregivers for their chicks. Males build nests on the ground. Then they sit on the eggs for 8 weeks. After the eggs hatch, males care for the chicks for about 18 months.

Ostriches are the largest birds in the world. They live in Africa. They can't fly either.

Mallee Fowls

Mallee fowls make crazy—and smelly—nests! Males build huge mounds of *compost*, or rotting vegetation. Females lay their eggs in the mounds.

The compost gives off heat. This keeps the eggs warm. To make sure the nests are the right temperature, males stick their tongues into the mounds to test them.

Kookaburras

Kookaburras' calls sound like loud laughs. But there's nothing funny about what these birds are trying to say.

They are warning other kookaburras to keep out of their territories.

Kookaburras are about 17 inches long. Insects, mice, and small snakes are their main food.

Southern Cassowaries

Cassowaries have hard spikes on their heads called *casques*. These flightless birds use their casques to dig into the ground. They're looking for fallen fruit to eat.

Many birds live in large groups, or *flocks*. But southern cassowaries don't. These birds live by themselves most of the time. They only live with other cassowaries when they are looking for mates or raising their chicks.

Ground Parrots

Ground parrots can fly. But they don't get far. They usually go just a few hundred feet before landing. That's why these parrots spend most of their time on the ground!

Ground parrots are nocturnal. Most of their enemies aren't active at night. That means it's safer for them to be out then.

Lyrebirds are part of a family of birds called *passiforms*. Family ancestors lived 20 million years ago. They may even be related to dinosaurs.

Lyrebirds make lots of crazy sounds. Some are copied from other birds. Males make whirring sounds when they mate with females. When they are frightened, lyrebirds make a *chuck*, *chuck* sound.

Kiwis

For thousands of years, no large mammals lived in New Zealand. That made it safe for birds to live in places where mammals usually live. So New Zealand is home to many flightless birds. These birds were able to nest and live on the ground without fear of enemies.

Kiwis are some of New Zealand's flightless birds. Not only can't they fly, but they don't even look or act like most other birds. Their feathers look more like fur. And they live in underground burrows instead of nests.

Keas are a type of parrots. They are so curious, they often get into trouble. They have been known to eat hikers' boots and tear up campers' tents! And their nosy behavior also helps them find new food sources in their harsh, cold home.

Keas may seem crazy. But scientists think they are some of the smartest birds in the world.

Kakapos are the only parrots in the world that cannot fly. They have small wings. But they only use their wings to glide down from trees.

Even though they can't fly, these birds can run very fast. And they are good at climbing trees!

Another crazy thing about kakapos is their size. These birds are the heaviest parrots in the world. Males weigh almost 9 pounds.

Kakapos are also the only land birds that can store fat in their bodies.

Chapter 5

Reptiles and Amphibians

Reptiles and amphibians are cold-blooded animals. That means their bodies are the same temperature as the air around them. They can't control their body temperatures. So if cold-blooded animals get too hot or too cold, they will die.

These animals keep warm by staying in the sun. They cool off by moving into the shade, crawling under rocks, or going for swims.

Reptiles and amphibians don't give birth to live young. Instead, they lay eggs. These animals usually lay many eggs at a time.

Reptiles and amphibians usually don't take care of their young. As soon as the eggs hatch, the babies are able to find food and take care of themselves.

Reptiles and amphibians are a lot alike. But there's one big difference between these two kinds of animals. Amphibians live in water when they are young. They breathe through gills. Reptiles are born with lungs.

When they become adults, amphibians' bodies change. Adult amphibians live on land. Then they breathe air through lungs.

Tuataras

Tuataras look a lot like dinosaurs. They are part of a group of reptiles that lived during the dinosaur age. New Zealand was cut off from the rest of the world. So no animals hunted tuataras. That's why this species was able to survive.

The males' crazy-looking spines gave these animals their name. *Tuatara* means "peaks on the back" in the Maori language.

Maoris were the first people to live on New Zealand.

These spines aren't just for show. Males can raise these spines to scare off other animals.

Frilled Lizards

These reptiles have a crazy way of scaring off enemies. They flip open a flap of skin around their necks. These flaps, or *frills*, make the lizards look much bigger and scarier than they really are.

Frilled lizards also have a crazy way of moving. Unlike other lizards, they often stand up on their back legs and run very fast. They are also good at climbing trees.

Blue-Tongued Skinks

These lizards really do have bright blue tongues! When they are in danger, they stick out their colorful tongues and hiss loudly. This helps scare away their enemies.

Skinks have another unusual way of defending themselves. Their heads and tails look a lot alike. This confuses their enemies. They can't figure out which end to attack. What a crazy way to stay safe!

Thorny Devils

Thorny devils are strange-looking lizards. The hard spikes on their bodies are like suits of armor. The spikes protect these reptiles from enemies.

Thorny devils live where it's hot and dry. But they never drink! Their skins are covered with tiny grooves. During the night, dew collects on the lizards' skins. The dew then runs down the grooves into the animals' mouths.

Geckos' bodies are very flat. They don't cast shadows as they stand very still on tree trunks. The color of a gecko's skin also blends in with the color of trees. Crazy tricks like these hide geckos from their enemies.

Geckos have very long, strange tongues. They can lick their own eyes!

Geckos' feet are very sticky. Hairy pads on their toes help them cling to any surface. They can even walk upside-down across ceilings!

Saurian crocodiles are the largest crocodiles in Australia. These fierce reptiles can grow up to 20 feet long!

Crocodiles are heavy. Their legs are very short. This makes it hard for them to walk on land. So they spend most of their time in water.

Crocodiles are great swimmers. They use their long, muscular tails to push themselves through the water.

Crocodiles can be very fierce. They eat almost anything—even people! These crazy animals are some of the fiercest predators on earth.

Water-Holding Frogs

Like all amphibians, most frogs need a constant supply of
water to survive. But these crazy frogs don't! Water-holding
frogs live where there are periods of hot, dry weather. They
survive the dry spells by storing water inside their bodies.
Some of these frogs can hold half their own weight in water.

Water-holding frogs also produce special layers of wet
skin that surround their bodies. Then they dig homes
underground. They sleep there until the rains come. They
can go for years before
waking up.

Chapter 6

Insects and Spiders

Insects are small animals that are part of a group called *arthropods*. Arthropods don't have backbones. They have jointed legs, segmented bodies, and hard shells called *exoskeletons*.

An insect's body is divided into three parts. There are the head; the *thorax*, or chest; and the *abdomen*, or stomach. Most insects also have six legs, two antennae, and four wings.

Spiders are part of the arthropod family too. But their bodies are different. Spiders have eight legs. And their bodies are divided into two parts, not three. Finally, spiders have fangs and poison glands.

Many unusual spiders and insects live in Australia and New Zealand. Let's meet a few of these crazy creatures.

Wetas

Birds aren't the only flightless creatures on New Zealand. These islands are also home to a flightless cricket!

Wetas use their wings only to communicate. They "sing" by rubbing their wings together. Males use their songs to attract mates.

Queen Alexandra's Birdwing Butterflies

Imagine butterflies as big as birds! Queen Alexandra's birdwings are the largest butterflies in the world. Their wingspans are almost a foot wide.

Because of their size and beauty, many people have killed and collected birdwings. So Queen Alexandra's birdwings are some of the rarest butterflies in the world.

Funnel-Web Spiders

Funnel-web spiders spin very strange webs. They spread large sheets of silky threads on the ground. Below the sheets, they build funnel-shaped webs.

The spiders hide at the bottom of the funnels. When insects or small animals land on the top part of the web, the spiders run up the funnels to catch them.

Funnel-web spiders kill their prey by injecting poison from their fangs. They are among the deadliest spiders in the world. They can kill animals much larger than themselves. Funnel-web spiders can kill people with one bite!

Chapter 7

Water Life

Many animals live in water. Some live in the salty ocean. Others live in freshwater lakes, ponds, streams, and rivers.

Animals that live in water have special body parts. Probably the strangest thing is that they don't breathe air with lungs. Instead, many water animals breathe underwater using gills.

Australia and New Zealand are surrounded by ocean water. They also have many lakes, ponds, streams, and rivers. Let's meet some of the crazy creatures that call these waters home.

Cleaner fish eat from the bodies of larger fish—and no one gets hurt. They eat parasites that live on other fish. They also eat dead scales from the bodies of other fish. These actions help both fish. Cleaner fish get good meals. And the other fish stay clean and healthy.

Why don't larger fish eat cleaner fish when they come near? Cleaner fish do special dances to tell other fish not to harm them.

Crown-of-Thorns Starfish

Crown-of-thorns starfish live on the Great Barrier Reef. This is a huge coral reef made of limestone. It is just off the coast of Australia.

Starfish have a crazy way of eating. They don't use their mouths. Instead, they eat with their stomachs! They push their stomachs out through their mouths. Then they digest their prey on the spot.

Crown-of-thorns starfish have caused a lot of damage to the Great Barrier Reef. It's a concern that they might eat their way right through the coral reef.

Weedy Sea Dragons

These sea creatures look like pieces of seaweed. But they are really fish! Rough pieces of skin hang from the weedy sea dragons' bodies. This makes them look like floating plants. Enemies can't see these disguised sea dragons.

Weedy sea dragons are a type of seahorses. Like other seahorses, male sea dragons care for the eggs. They carry them in special pouches on their bodies.

Kouras

These animals are also called freshwater crayfish. They live in streams, lakes, and ponds.

Even though they live in water, kouras don't need to stay wet to live. If the water dries up, kouras dig deep into the mud. They wait there until the water returns.

Kouras don't have to look too hard for food. They eat bits of leaves and other food that floats in the water or sinks to the bottom.

Kouras are covered with hard shells. As they get bigger, the shells become too small. Finally, the shells split open. Then kouras will crawl out wearing new shells.

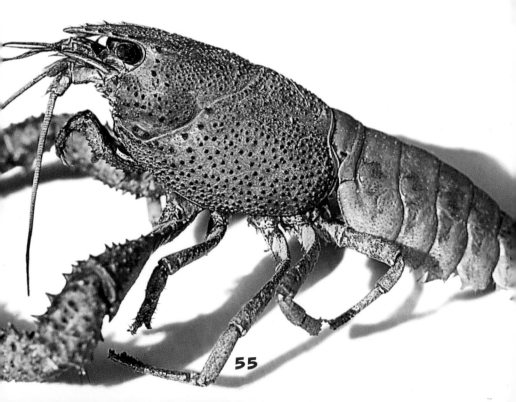